There's More In YOU!

Breaking Free From The Chains That Keep You Bound

Karona Wilson

Copyright © 2016 by Karona Wilson

All Rights Reserved. No part of this publication may be reproduced in any form or by any means, including scanning, photocopying, or otherwise without prior written permission from the author.

ISBN: 978-0-692-68246-3

To order additional copies of this book, contact
the author: Karona Wilson

Email: kayewilsonr@gmail.com
Website: www.theresmoreinyou.com

Edited by: Dr. Margena Christian
Website: www.margenachristian.com

Published by: Karona Wilson

Photography by: Cory Lampkin Productions
Website: www.corylampkinproductions.com

Printed in the United States of America in 2016

The Lord will perfect that which concerns me.

~ Psalms 138:8a~

Break the chains from your mind.

There's More In YOU.

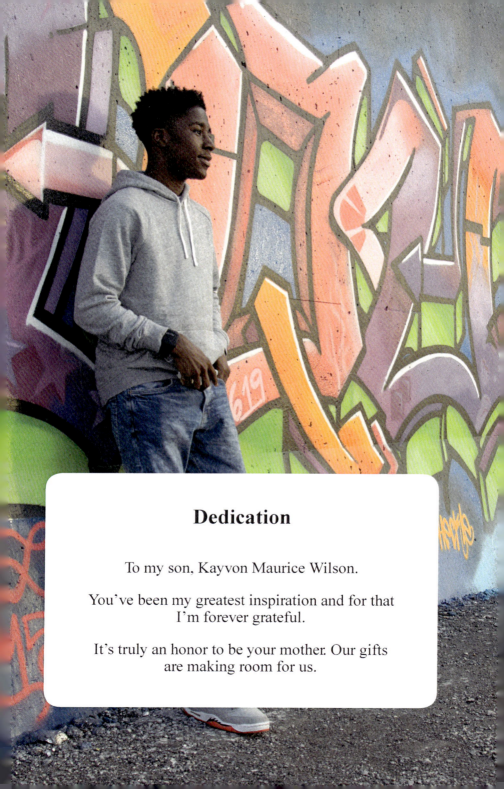

Dedication

To my son, Kayvon Maurice Wilson.

You've been my greatest inspiration and for that I'm forever grateful.

It's truly an honor to be your mother. Our gifts are making room for us.

I Salute YOU!

I would like to express my gratitude to the following:

My Lord and Savior, Jesus Christ, who saved me and set me FREE from all that had me bound! I'm forever grateful for his love toward me.

To my mother, Karen Wilson, for the love, support, and for always being in my corner. To my dad, Fredrick Jay Wilson, I thank God for the shift that has taken place in our relationship. To my siblings, for believing in me and watching me grow. You loved me through it all. To my entire family, thank you for your love and support throughout the years.

To my Naomi-godmom (Eneazer Layne), thank you for always extending your love and paving the way for me as well. A.L. Layne, my godfather, thank you for being my warrior and example of what a man should exhibit. Aunt Fontella Wiggins, I thank you for pushing me into my wealthy place. My grandmother, Eloise Stanton, your love toward me is priceless and I'm forever grateful. To Anna Simpson, Shannon Thompson, Amber Moore, Kimberly Bell, Stephanie Jordan and Roshonda Epps, your honesty and trust have been the pillar to my journey.

To Pastor Ron and Lady Dorretta Stephens, thank you for your integrity, prayers, support, love, and heart to serve.

In addition, I would like to extend my appreciation to everyone who has impacted my life over the years. I truly appreciate the support and encouragement throughout my journey.

Anna Lee Wilson, who is now in heaven, thank you for believing in me at the age of 5. You taught me the quality of life and how to trust God no matter what.

Last but not least, I would like to express my love and appreciation to everyone who said I would not succeed. Thanks for pushing me into my destiny!

Table of Contents

Dedication	5
I Salute YOU!	6
INTRODUCTION	10
THE MASK	11
CHAPTER 1 The Beginning	14
CHAPTER 2 It's Hard Changing Your Life	24
CHAPTER 3 Who Are You to You?	27
CHAPTER 4 How I Knew I Was at My Breaking Point?	30
CHAPTER 5 Just Do It!	36
CHAPTER 6 Focus on You	42
CHAPTER 7 Your Moment	45
Prayer, Scriptures, and References	47
Thank You Letters	55
Dear God	59
Moments of Reflections	60
About the Author	121

Introduction

THE MASK

Whether you are held bound by your thinking, your upbringing, your relationships, or whatever it may be, you have the power within you to BREAK FREE! Freedom was given to us by God so take a stand. Never again will you allow anyone to put a harness of slavery on you. Stand fast therefore in the liberty by which Christ has made us free, and do not be entangled again with a yoke of bondage. **<u>Galatians 5:1</u> <u>NKJV</u>**

We can become imprisoned by our own comfort zone. Our comfort zone can keep us from experiencing all that God has for us and it could stunt our growth. **<u>There's More In You.</u>**

These are some principles that will help you on your journey:

- Know God's will for your life will be fulfilled.

- Know you must step out on faith.

- Know you can't allow fear to stop you.

- Know there are times your journey will cause you to feel uncomfortable.

Don't focus on the problem. **GET OUT OF THE BOAT AND BREAK FREE.** Your life story is designed to strengthen someone to pursue his/her dreams. You have fought to tear down the wall of destruction for the next generation to come and you are **<u>necessary.</u>**

Don't allow the abuses of your past to keep you from pushing forward to your destiny. The art of you is pouring out a fresh stream of new possibilities. What lies within you? Is it a book? A movie? A school? A ministry? A heart to give? To serve? You are a profound soul. Make your impact on the world. Without your touch, we would miss out on **THE BETTER YOU!**

One day I decided I was tired of not pursuing the knowledge of the truth of ME! So I started praying and talking to God to understand what I had to offer Him and the world. I became a new person in HIM by breaking away from my old habits, ways, places, relationships, organizations, and broke the chains from my mind through HIS word.

The questions are, how do you stay free? It's a never-ending conscience effort to stay connected to Him. Who are you connected to? Do they hold you accountable? What's feeding you? I had to re-examine my lifestyle and relationships. Remember, everything that we have to face has already been nailed to the cross.

I pray that my story inspires you to pursue the better YOU through HIM for HIM.

You are a step away from the view of the other side of your life. There's More In You!

In this book, I share with you my journey to the road of freedom. I had to disconnect in order to reconnect. What are you willing to let go of to walk with God and experience spiritual freedom?

What stopped me from being FREE?

F- FRUSTRATION, FAILURE, FEAR, FRAGILE, AND FORGOTTEN

R- REJECTION, REVENGE, RAGE, REGRET, AND RESENTMENT

E- ENVY, ENTANGLED, ENRAGED, ENSLAVED, AND EMOTIONALLY BANKRUPT

E- EXHAUSTION, EMBARRASSMENT, AND EMPTINESS

How I broke FREE

F- FAITH, FORGIVENESS, FULFILLMENT, FEARLESSNESS, AND FRUITFULNESS

R- RESTORATION, REFRESHNESS, RESILIENCE, REBIRTH, AND REST

E- EMBRACE, ENOUGH, ENRICHED, ENCOURAGED, AND EXTRAORDINARY

E- ESSENTIAL, EQUIPPED, ESTEEM, EMPOWERED, AND ENDOWED

What chains are holding you down? The power within you is greater than what is around you. Tap into the better YOU! There will never be another you in this entire world. You were created on purpose to live your life with purpose. What is God's purpose for your life?

There's more In YOU.

CHAPTER 1

The Beginning

The Beginning

It was nine months that produced the life of my soul. The day of me was approaching. She's here! There's a lot of bright lights that surfaced and people were smiling at me. I took my first breath and the art of my life began. All the family was there to see me, hold me, kiss me, change me, and love on me. I am sure I was crying because of hunger or wanting to be held.

When I was a toddler, I can remember the moments I learned how to crawl and now I'm walking, getting into everything I could possibly think of and tearing up everything that's in reach. The composition of my mind was learning the other side of me. Now all the people who were smiling at me, kissing me, holding me, and loving on me are now spanking my hands because I had learned there was much more to me.

Book bags, crayons, pencils, erasers, lunch bags, homework, etc. were a part of my responsibilities. The core of being a carefree little girl was being stripped from me too soon. The resemblance of an adult was being birthed and I had no clue. In life, we are all dealt cards that impact our lives. I dreamed of a white picket fence, a two-parent household, a dog, and a quiet neighborhood. I would say I was dreaming of a family like the ones shown on TV series such as *Leave it to Beaver* (1957-1963) and The Cosby Show (1984-1992). These were shows I enjoyed as a kid. I had this thought of a perfect family. I recall as a little girl asking my mom, "Mom, do you ever wonder why you have the parents you have?" With a disturbing look, she said, "Yes, I do. That's the way God wanted it to be sweetie."

I was so curious. I would watch shows and see my friends from school with both parents. My little mind couldn't comprehend what was taking place in my life. I remember, at the age of 5, I took a crayon and paper and wrote a letter to God about what I saw. The next day I put it in an envelope and when I saw the mailman I gave it to him.

He said, "What is this, little lady?"

I asked him, "Could you please send this letter to God?"

He chuckled and said, "I don't think I can, but I'll try to get it to Him." He then got serious and stated, "Little lady, you should pray to HIM."

I said, "What's that?"

He said, "It's a conversation you have with HIM."

By that time, I was even more confused. So, the next day I was going over my granny's house and asked her, "How do you pray?"

She looked at me with a glare in her eyes and smiled. My granny was so beautiful. She had a fair complexion with soft skin, and she always smelled like cocoa butter.

I can hear her voice saying, "Baby, come here. It's time we have a conversation. Prayer is when you have a conversation with God. You talk to Him about you and he hears and answers you. God is everywhere. He's here now."

Again, my little mind could not get this, but if my granny said so, I'm going to believe it. We kneeled down to pray and then I learned the Lord's Prayer!

After this manner, therefore, pray ye:

Our Father which art in heaven, Hallowed be thy name.

Thy kingdom come, Thy will be done in earth, as it is in heaven. Give us this day our daily bread.

And forgive us our debts, as we forgive our debtors.

And lead us not into temptation, but deliver us from evil: For thine is the kingdom, and

The power, and the glory, forever. Amen.

I was so excited I learned how to pray.

I loved going to my granny's house because sometimes it was just me and her . We traveled, shopped, planted vegetables and fruits. She showed me unconditional love.

I also learned how to cook and prepare healthy meals. I couldn't understand why my granny was teaching me how to do all of these things as if I was an adult. You never know what you are being prepared for. There is always a lesson to be learned in life. Pay attention to the details. My granny was an advocate on eating healthy and the importance of taking care of your body. Going to her house and having to face the reality of going back home was so confusing.

We had different struggles at home. There were a consistent flow of drugs, prostitution, killing, and many other forms of activities taking place in our neighborhood. To o be at my granny's house was a breath of fresh air for me as a kid. From a newborn to a toddler, to daycare, preschool, elementary, middle school, and then high school, it was a storm of a life I had to endure. We all have to transition with or without direction. We have to go to the next level of life. Have you ever wondered, "How can I get out of this place? Who can I talk to when I feel alone and rejected by just about everyone I know? Who will care about me and how I feel? If I share my feelings with them, would they tell someone? I'm afraid to open up to my pastor, my friends, my loved ones, or anyone for that matter. Every time I do, I end up with darts in my back. Why is that?"

With the many things we face daily, it could be challenging to break free from the expectations of the world or from the bondage that has you trapped. You may feel frustrated, rejected, enslaved,

empty, embarrassed, and not good enough. You want to do anything that will help you to break free from your past.

I used to keep everything balled up because of things I discovered in my childhood or early adulthood. As a kid, I used to keep silent because I never thought I was good enough. I was not the "cute light-skinned skinny little girl" with the long, pretty hair. I wasn't the world's perspective of what we should look like. I was "chunky" with slanted eyes. I never smiled because I didn't have anything to smile about. I was raised in single parent household. My mother struggled with mental and health problems. Now, granted my mother did the best she could with the tools she was given and she did a great job! My dad was inconsistent in my life. We grew up in poverty. I very seldom heard the words **I LOVE YOU**. As I look back, it wasn't because my mom didn't love me, but she was struggling with previous abuse from her past relationships. My mother would cry out to God every night for help. She loved my siblings and me. However, I noticed the love she needed was inconsistent from her father. It was God's love that drew her closer to us and HIM.

At the age of 12, I immediately learned the meaning of being an adult. My mom became ill with a condition that the doctors could not identify. I would be at home with my little brother and sister, taking care of them. I protected them like a mom would. I cooked, helped with homework, played outside, and had to fight kids off of them. My mom was diagnosed with numerous illnesses such as lupus, a thyroid condition, arthritis, and much more. She sacrificed her life for all four of us, even though my baby brother stayed with his dad. I knew my mother loved us.

As I grew older, I realized my mom was a woman who was bruised, mistreated, manipulated, taken for granted, and misplaced. She raised us while she was going through a healing process herself.

As time proceeded, I would seek out love in all of the wrong places. The love would come from the TV shows, friends, or a boyfriend. Years later it occured to me I was searching for my dad in them. I always dreamed of being a daddy's girl. I loved my daddy, in spite of his shortcomings. I really didn't see any wrong in him because of my love for him. He was bruised indeed! One broken by the weight of sorrow, or care, or sin. He would promise to pick us up and most times would never show up. When he did this, we would always cry and he left us hopeless.

I remember watching my mom become so angry as she watched us cry. She didn't like seeing us hurt like that. My parents married at a very young age and my mother kept her virginity until marriage. They later divorced after my little brother was born. My dad was searching for himself and at that time fighting many demons, which caused him to later turn to drugs and alcohol. A man God called to create a life of purpose and ministry was being controlled by the weight of this world. Again, I never saw his flaws. I only saw what I wanted and that was my daddy, no matter how many times he failed me. I believed in him before he believed in himself. I wanted my siblings to think like me, but that was not not logical nor a reality to them.

The seed of God was sowed in me by my aunt, both of my grandmothers, and a few others who showed their love toward me. Just when you think everything is crashing down on you, God always provides a way of escape. They would hold me tight on nights when I was scared and wondered if I would ever see my mom. As a kid, I always heard that my mom was sick and in the hospital. I was feeling hopeless because I did not know what was going to happen next. The kids at school knew about my mother and would say cruel things that hurt me. I felt like I was always defending my siblings and myself because of this type of bullying. I remember fighting this person and that person off my siblings because of the mean things they would say to them. I can laugh now because I was really a little Mike Tyson or Muhammad Ali as a kid.

I remember being so angry because my granny came to the house to let us know that our mom would have to stay in the hospital longer than expected. I was mad! My duties as an adult at a young age were prolonged. At the time I received this news, my brother and sister were outside playing. I was already cooking and doing my homework.

All of a sudden my brother came into the house crying. He told me, "She hit me and said mom was going to die!" I said, "Who?" I ran outside boiling inside. Now, as a reminder, I am only 12. I went to the little girl and struck her in the face. Her brother tried to jump in, but I hit him in the face, too. At that moment, I felt adrenaline in my body of hatred. I was so angry and mad that I was scared of what could happen next. Their dad came outside and asked me to stop beating his kids. I shouted, "Don't ever mess with my brother again!"

Thank God I've been delivered!

Welcome Home

It was weeks before my mom finally returned home. I would hear my mom cry out to God to take her because the load of life had become too heavy to bear.

My mom was a single parent of four and all she dreamed of for her life was fading away. She had to make a decision of what was important at the time. She pleaded with God by saying, "Why me and how did this happen? Take care of my babies, Lord! Allow me to live to see my babies live their lives."

My Life Changed

Knowing and unknowingly, I would seek the approval for friendship of others. Going into my sophomore year in high school was a challenging moment for me. I was trying to relive the time I lost as a kid, but it was too late for that. In my mind, I thought maybe everyone would accept me if I was nice or gave them what they wanted. Well, life doesn't work like that.

****NEWS FLASH****

It's a tragedy when two hurting people connect, especially, when you are not aware of your brokenness, you tend to destroy each another.

After completing my second year in high school and approaching my junior year, my life changed. I started dating my high school love and he showered me with love and gifts. I was head over hills and I just knew this was the best person for me. In March 1999, all I ever dreamed of was shattered and destroyed. I found out I was five months pregnant. I was at a loss for words. Along with that, I had applied to enlist in U.S. Navy.

WHAT AM I GOING TO DO? WHAT, KARONA?! YOU COULD BARELY FEED YOURSELF!

The moment of truth came. I had to tell my family. I struggled for three weeks with this decision and thinking I can't continue to hide my pregnancy any longer. I told my boyfriend and he denied that I was carrying his baby. So, I had an even **BIGGER** issue.

My next stop was to tell my mom. I was nervous because all I could think was what am I going to do? Not to mention my grandmother was ill and she had high hopes for me. When I told my mom, she stated, "You laid in that bed, so you will make it."

Now my mind was racing. "What are you going to do, Karona? How do you plan to take care of this child?" The options I was pondering were abortion or adoption. I couldn't imagine someone else taking care of my baby. So, my new options were to either have an abortion or have the baby. I decided to sleep on it and once I thought about it further, I couldn't abort my child. I started feeling my baby moving along with pain and tears filled my eyes. "I don't know how I'm going to care for this baby, but I know I can't be responsible for this baby's death!" At that moment, I spoke with my granny and as I listened to the disappointment in her voice, "It won't be easy, but with God on your side, you will be ok." I just knew that everything that I thought of pursuing was over with. Well, so I thought. I was scared as heck.

In July 1999, the month of my baby shower, my granny informed me she was getting very sick. I was thinking it was just a cold because my granny was so healthy and she never got sick. By October 9, 1999, my granny's health was rapidly declining. She was diagnosed early with lung cancer and learned it had spread throughout her entire body. I can never forget the conversation I had with her at 10:00 p.m. that day. I called her to let her know I had not given birth yet and she said to me:

"Baby, it's ok. I already know how he looks. He's going to have a head full of hair and look just like you. Just put my name in their somewhere, baby. Life is going to get hard and it's not going to be easy, but promise me this… DON'T QUIT! I love you and I'm proud of you, baby. Keep God First!"

There is no more suffering for my granny. She is in the bosom of the Lord now. She prepared me for her exit and prepared me for my life. All I could hear her say is, **"DON'T QUIT!"**

Life After

Continuing along this journey I'm now living with my mom, my little sister and my brother in a 4-bedroom apartment in the inner city. Our apartment was infested with rodents and I'm having a baby soon. Now, during the same time my child's father was very abusive verbally, physically, mentally, and emotionally. I realized years later he was a broken child, crying out for HELP.

Two days after my granny's death, I gave birth to a healthy baby boy. Wow, at 17 years old I was a mom! I just knew my life was over and all my dreams and aspirations were gone or so I thought. My circle of friends changed and my son's dad became more inconsistent. We were both young and lost. Babies having a baby. A single mom with no transportation, no job, living in some uncomfortable situations and also living off of government assistance. I remember walking down the street with my son on my hip on a cold day. There was snow on the ground and it was sleeting and raining as well. I was walking when tears filled my eyes, carrying a diaper bag and a book bag. I missed the bi-state bus and I was pissed. What a day! Everyone I called for a ride to get home was unavailable.

****NEWS FLASH****

What you think is a curse is a blessing to your destiny. God is preparing you for what's ahead. Don't discount the process of life. It's in the dark places that will develop and prepare you for your journey.

I yelled, "LORD, WHEN WOULD LIFE GET BETTER?" As I cried, keep in my mind my son is having a ball. This helped ease the pain. As I looked at him, I realized: Use the time to build memories and make this an adventure. Embrace what you consider a bad situation and make it the best moments of your life. It was at that moment when I realized how blessed I really was.

CHAPTER 2

It's Hard Changing Your Life

It's Hard Changing Your Life

Change is a word that we tend to avoid. I believe it challenges us to come out of our comfort zone. In Chapter 1, I shared my story of how I grew up and the generational situations that occurred. Change was important for me to learn that I could no longer be the victim.

The chains that keep you bound to the past are not the actions of another person. They are your own anger, stubbornness, lack of compassion, jealousy and blaming others for your choices. It is not other people that keep you trapped; it is the entitled role of victim that you enjoy wearing. There is a familiarity to pain that you enjoy because you get a payoff from it. When you figure out what that payoff is, then you will finally be on the road to freedom.

It was time for me to change my life and I knew it was not going to be easy. I endured years of pain, so I knew I could not change on my own. I want you to know that it is going to take something higher than you to get through the change process. Seeking people, places, and things will not cut it. I know this because instead of seeking God first, I would think I could trust other people with my personal business. I had to learn after many attempts to allow God to do the connecting and trust Him. We put our trust in people and that's not divine order. The Bible says, "It is better to take refuge in the LORD than to trust in man." (Psalm 118:8 ESV) If you can't trust the leadership of your leader, you need to pray for direction and wisdom for a shift change.

I decided one day that I was tired of being locked up in my own prison, one I created for myself. I held in my dreams, aspirations, visions, or things that I saw because I didn't believe in myself nor did I believe it was possible. I would see everyone else accomplish his/her goals and envy that person. I never once thought that I could do it because they had the ability to do it. Maybe I was being intimidated by my own potential and seeing the loin of greatest rising within me. The fear of success and the road to works of greatness would scare me.

I pushed other people's vision, ministry, and encouraged them but I was left empty. Are you encouraging everyone else and leaving yourself empty? Are you ashamed of who you are or who you are trying to become because of lack of knowledge? Are you jealous of someone else because of how she/he looks or how she/he speaks?

****NEWS FLASH****

Please understand it's very important to sow into someone's vision but make sure it's spirit led.

This was the old Karona. I had to change my life by focusing on what God had planned for me That was what God placed in me all alone. It was just dormant. I tapped into what had been in me from the beginning of time. It was so much trying to block me from my purpose. I had to do some cleaning up inside. This started by being real with myself and not telling everyone else about me, but telling me about me. I looked into the mirror and began to talk to my soul. It was an hour of cleansing and laying on my floor in the dark, waiting. At one moment, I stopped and just let God talk to me. I was going through a major healing process. A night with my friend, my healer, my deliverer, and my Savior. Most importantly, He would never share what was said in that sacred moment. My eyes of my understanding were opened and I could see me the way God saw me.

Change is an ongoing process, but it's possible and it's worth it.

CHAPTER 3

Who Are You to You?

Who Are You To You?

So many times I thought I had to explain who I was and why. I tried to speak up, but people would not give me the opportunity to speak or they would speak over me. I was tucking away my creativity to be who people wanted me to be. I poured more of my time into their vision and neglected what God had given me, which was a purpose to live, to dream and to believe in my own vision. I buried who I was created to become because of improper teaching.

Have you ever found yourself in a group setting, denying yourself because of the fear of what people think of you? I urge you to remove yourself from that environment and then move yourself into the right places to use your gifts. You are full of substance and the world needs YOU.

I recognized the abuse of certain people and it was evident it was a bad connection. The purpose they served in my life had been fulfilled and it was time to make a move immediately. The moment I broke from those relationships, BEHAVIORS, and places, I was able to do some soul searching and I found myself. Indeed, the day I removed the mask of the false reality of me was the day I met the new ME!

Do whatever it takes to change your life. I'm a living witness that you need to make a shift with God, not people. God is your source and He will provide what you need. Was this road easy for me? No. But I found out who was really there for me. In my dark place I met God on a new level. Just like the woman with the Alabaster box (Matthew 26:7 NIV) it was important that I gave HIM my all!

I would ask questions like, "Why do they speak against my life? Why do they say I went crazy?" Even when I tried to be mad, all I could do is pray and still love them. Why? It was because we all fall short of the glory of God. We've all said things that we wish we could take back. The best thing for me was to forgive and forget. It was the spirit of God that prevailed within me that allowed me to extend my love no matter how hurt I was.

The next time someone speaks negative toward you, remember it's a reflection of who that person is and forgive him/her. Extend compassion, grace, mercy, and most of all LOVE.

Know who you are to you. There's a new you that is about to come out. When I found myself, I knew I was a woman full of substance who is unstoppable.

CHAPTER 4

How I Knew I Was at My Breaking Point?

How Did I Know I Was At My Breaking Point?

Listen, don't believe every spirit. Test the spirit by the spirit (1 John 4:1). Why is this important? Testing the spirit means that one must know how to examine others. It's important to not believe in everything you hear. It is either the doctrine of God or the doctrine of demons. Not everything or everyone is of God. The Holy Spirit would give us a clear indication of what is from God. Use your instincts and trust your gut. Vibes don't lie. The beauty and the art of your soul are so delicate and important that you don't have time to feed it to wolves.

How to get into your zone and stay in your lane?

How could I do this? Will this ever happen to me? In re-evaluating myself, I realized I was connected to the WRONG PEOPLE.

****NEWS FLASH****

Please understand the importance of being connected to the right people along your journey and it may change.

In the past, my circle became very draining over time. I thought something was wrong with me since the people in my circle made me feel bad. They had me tripping like I was wrong about what I was feeling inside of me. Um, not. For more than five years I was mishandled by people I admired. I valued their direction and wisdom for my life. In reality, I stayed too long.

There comes a time when God has given you the okay to leave. When this happens, please do yourself a favor and GO! I became so uncomfortable and out of character that foolishness was my environment. It was an environment that I condoned. Really, I was. Foolishness became my environment.

One day, in July 2013, I was sitting in a conference when it hit me that I had to go. I was committing spiritual suicide and it was no one's fault but my own. I saw the faces of my enemies and it shocked me. I went back to my room and cried because I was stunned. You must put your trust in God and He will guide you if you let Him. In that moment, I felt betrayed and witnessed trust being diminished. My personal thoughts, conversations, and information were being shared like I didn't matter. How could they do this to me?

God spoke to me and said, "I handpicked you to be afflicted." I was confused. He told me that they were assigned to afflict me and it was a step to push me into my destiny. I was angry for a while but when God told me to fast and pray for them, I was thinking, "Really??" That's when I had an "Ah-Ha" moment. This whole time it's been about God. God said those are my children and as my child I need you to intercede for your siblings. You are built for this. When you walk away, it'll hurt but know you will survive and thrive.

Now truthfully I was thinking to myself, "God, you could've picked someone else." As a believer, we all have experienced some level of betrayal. It could have been someone in your family, people at your job, your church, or even your inner circle of so-called friends. Remember that everyone has an assignment. Allow them to do what they've been called to do in your life. It will either break you or make you better.

After I had gotten over my feelings, I could not resist the spirit that was laying so heavy on me to make the right decision: LOVE THEM IN SPITE OF THE SITUATION. No matter what was said about me, I had to make peace with the situation and most importantly I had to forgive them for me. Yes, FORGIVENESS. Forgiveness is something we run from because we love to hold on to things. Why? It gives us power, or so we think. Forgiveness is me giving up my right to hurt you for hurting me. You do not have to be the victim in the situation. Release, forgive and love on the people .

You have not always been where you are. We are all striving to be better. I don't recommend you to go back to those relationships or places where you once were . But, what I am encouraging you to do is let it go because there will come a time when you may have to embrace them and be authentic. Be bigger and be better.

Your obedience to God may cause your foes or enemies to change. Now, they may never tell you that, but you must allow your fruit to show. God has freed me from all of that. Amen. I'm forever indebted to HIM. God has transformed me.

God loves us all. He has forgotten about all the hurt we have caused Him. So, why do we struggle with loving on those who despitefully use us? Now, again I am not telling you to go back into those relationships. I just want you to know that you can love them with no resentment and still live freely. I am a living witness.

The Letter

Two years ago I wrote a letter to the people who loved me through one of the rough times in my life. It read the following:

Dear Family,

When I was at my low, you were there. When I had to move with no place to go you were there. You rubbed my back and reminded me of the love that God has for me. He's still with me. You made sure I went church, even when I didn't want to go. You called me every day and gave me a scripture and prayed with me. You were patient with me. You invited me to dinner and worked out with me. You helped me to change my way of eating spiritually and physically.

You helped me not to look at all church leaders as bad people. You informed me they were in need of prayer just like me. You showed me how to love on another level. You helped me when my mom had a stroke. You pushed me even when I couldn't push for myself. I was crunched up in the basement of my mom's house with my 13-year-old son. You informed me this was just a valley experience. You wouldn't allow me to consume my mind with the fact that they were laughing at me because it looked like I made a bad move. You believed in the woman I was becoming before I met her. You saw her and loved the new her before I knew her. I love you with all my heart! You are always in my heart. I pray God would bless your life and I've watched God take you from here to there. And, I love you forevermore. To my destiny I love you and we are getting closer than ever.

When God is shifting your life, do not waste your time in unnecessary places. Here's a way to identify if you are connected to the right people. Find out the following: What's their purpose in your life? Are they sharpening you (Proverbs 27:17) and vice versa? You would know them by their fruits. Also, is it from God? Beware of false prophets, who come to you in sheep's clothing, but inwardly they are ravenous wolves (Matthew 7:15).

In October 2014, I attended Bishop T.D. Jakes' "Woman Thou Art Loosed Conference" and Pastor Van Moody was one of the guest speakers. Pastor Moody stated, "People are either your armor-bearer or pall-bearer. They're either taking you to your destiny or taking you to your grave!" These people are both necessary but in its own time.

Bishop T.D. Jakes said, "You must surround yourself with those who won't compete with but will revel in your success and see it as a reflection of their own possibilities." Surround yourself around those that would push you into your destiny. There is great strength in small numbers when the people involved are strong in the Lord! The quality of your relationships is more important than the quantity. (The Power Of A Praying Woman-Stormie Omartian) Pray for Godly people to come into your life with whom you can connect.

God is creating a team/relationship for your life. There are people waiting to hear you, know you, feel you, love you and embrace you. It's all up to YOU. You are so necessary. You have a purpose in life and it's to fulfill the destiny and the call that's on your life. It's time to shake all the naysayers, your past, negative talks, and negative people-false teaching (wolf in sheep's clothing) Matthew 7:15.

<u>YOU ARE A LIFE CHANGER AND THE WORLD IS WAITING TO MEET YOU.</u>

CHAPTER 5

Just Do It!

Just Do It!

Move quickly and don't wait to think about it, especially when God has given you the instructions. I remember reading Bishop T.D. Jakes' book *Instincts* and what stood out to me was "Follow your instincts." Simple, right? This literally woke me up! It's good to have faith but without work it means nothing. Take action and go!

Sometimes you may have to go through your journey alone. Stop trying to take people with you that are not assigned to you. In my case, I have a son and he was the only person I had to take with me. It's wasn't my responsibility to tag anyone else to go along with me. God was doing a new thing in me and it started in my dark place. He had a plan for me that no one could take credit for. He sent people to help me along the way (and I'm forever grateful), but it was always God. What has God called you to do?

Overthinking Junkie

In September 2015, I made the decision to stop overthinking everything. YUCK. I kept overreacting to every single situation. This led me to miss opportunities. I devoted too much time and thought to past hurts and disappointments. After the situation is exposed and healing begins, take action. What a tragic waste it is to not use or not maximize. Don't assume you have tomorrow. All you have for sure is right now. Take action now. NOW IS THE TIME.

Procrastination and overthinking can cause you to miss the opportunities God has for you. I was a huge procrastinator. I had to break free of my old self in order to seek the next opportunity by believing that a fulfilling, happy and peaceful life were possible. I had to make a decision and believe life was possible for Karona. Yes, I could live my dreams. I had put off so many opportunities, waiting on the perfect conditions. Now my team (accountable partners) pushes me to complete all my assignments and hold me accountable.

This is your time to take action and have faith, trust what God has for you . There may be a book, a weight loss, a business, a ministry, or a non-profit organization on your journey.

birthing inside of you. Only you can push this vision. God gave you this gift and the moment to pursue this gift seriously.

When I started my weight loss journey, the first thing I had to do was admit I needed to change my mindset. It's vital that you make changes and flow in the direction that your life is taking you. I knew if I wanted to really do what I've been called and equip to do. I needed to take my health seriously. I kept ignoring it and putting it off. I started exercising like a maniac, but my diet was all over the place. I felt a change in my body but I kept overlooking it. I was experiencing pain throughout my whole body. One day I couldn't resist it anymore and I went to the doctor.

During my first visit to the doctor, numerous tests were conducted. I was told my vitamin D levels were too low. So, I started taking vitamin tablets. I began to get dizzy more and more. One day while at work, I went to urgent care. I was diagnosed with Vertigo. Vertigo is a sensation of spinning and if you have these dizzy spells, you might feel like you are spinning or that the world around you is spinning. In my case, vertigo was caused by migraines.

Months went by and my body was still in a lot of pain. I had this goal to complete another 5k run. I heard that the Biggest Loser Race was coming to St. Louis. On the day of the race, I kept noticing the pain in my body and the exhaustion I was experiencing. While I was running at least 2 miles into the race, I became very dizzy and the pain got worse. I finished the race within 45 mins. It was an awesome achievement! However, I was still in pain. I overlooked the pain and kept running.

Within a month, I went back to the doctor. This time when the results came back and I was diagnosed with arthritis. Arthritis is very common but is not well understood. Actually, arthritis is not a single disease; it is an informal way of referring to joint pain or joint disease. Common arthritis joint symptoms include swelling, pain, stiffness and decreased range of motion. Symptoms may come and go. They can be mild, moderate or severe.

Two weeks later and I noticed how the pain got worse. I went back to the doctor and they ran more tests. The palms of my hands were sweaty and my heart was pounding. The doctor said, "Ms. Wilson, I'm sorry, but your report came back and it shows that you have Lupus." I wasn't expecting this. Lupus is a chronic inflammatory disease that occurs when your body's immune system attacks your own tissues and organs. The doctor's mouth was moving, but I could not tell you anything she said. I tuned her out. I was numb. My mom has Lupus and she's on numerous medications. I have seen how she suffers.

At that moment, I told God, "You have my undivided attention." I told my doctor to give me 6 months and I wouldn't need any medication. I was thinking, "They wouldn't see me anymore." She told me that I needed to change my diet. I should've started when God told me to stop procrastinating. If I would have followed His will, it's no telling what would've transpired.

My friend, who is also like a sister to me, connected me with some amazing trainers. During a phone consultation to one trainer, I explained that I had some medical issues and he immediately knew what it was. At that point, I knew this was it. I worked with a trainer to help with my meals and I participated in a weekly fitness routine. In six months, I created a new lifestyle for myself. I'm truly grateful for my trainer. He really pushed me to greater levels along this journey. Guess what? My new lifestyle rewarded me with losing more than 50 pounds.

I was consistent and determined to win. I had a made up mind to be a healthier me. You have to listen to your body. When I went back to the doctor, she couldn't believe my transition and how rapidly I had changed. Praise Report: I did not have to be on any medication and my blood work came back clear. She couldn't find anything! Praise God! While she did not understand, I did.

I recognized the why to this situation. My WHY statement was: "Take charge of your health because it's the key to your wealth!"

Do not wait until something tragic occurs in your life to get the attention of God. You are responsible for what you allow in your temple. In what area of your life do you need to make changes? Examine those hurdles and say, "I'll get back at it next week and I'll start that diet tomorrow. I will forgive them tomorrow. I'll cut those credit cards after Christmas. I'll tell them how I feel one day or I'll wait on them to tell me. I'll sign up for school. I'll tell my husband I love him tomorrow or vice versa. Whatever it may be, how long will you put it off?"

Imagine 10 years ago how God told you to do something. Now you have tubes down your throat, you are standing over the casket, you are watching him or her marry someone else. Now the interest rates are higher. What would've been free classes are now going to cost you double. Would you like to complete or start the task that has been prepared for you?

I recall asking God, "Are you telling me to write this book?" I wanted to wait until after my son graduated from high school. One day God said, "Destiny awaits for you." Your story must be told NOW. God had informed me that my destiny was in my story and my blessing was connected to my next move, so I had to be obedient.

We all face many challenges in life, but no matter what they may be, you have it in you to seize the opportunity. Write the vision and make it plain (Habakkuk 2:2). Discipline yourself to work your vision.

4 Steps to The Discipline Of Vision (Dr. Myles Munroe)

- Vision chooses your diet
- Vision chooses your to-do-list

- Vision chooses your attitude in life
- Vision chooses your life

Vision simplifies your life and it also helps to identify who you are. Use your energy to go after it as if your life depends on it. Don't seek success; seek to become a person of value. Make yourself valuable and watch how people desire to be near you. Free your mind of all the negative thoughts of who would listen, how would this work, where would the money come from. Just Do It and watch HIM work!

In November 2010, I started my business with $10.00 in my pocket. Yes, $10.00! I left a salon with a clientele, because I heard the voice of God saying it's time to move forward into your own business. Ever since that day I've seen HIM do some miraculous things through me and my business. Has it been easy? NO! But with God all things are possible. I believed even when I could not see. God provided the victory. I've owned my business for more than six years and I've been in the beauty industry for more than twelve years.

I had some issues and many challenges, but with God and the right team of people in my life I was able to do it and so can you! In His perfect timing, everything will come to pass.

You should create a vision board. Cut out pictures, write affirmations, feed your mind, and change your self-talk. Place your vision board in your home or at your workplace. You can break free from all the negative self-talk and walk into your divine purpose in life. So, what's your purpose? Develop a relationship with God and He will lead you according to HIS word. Surviving is not enough. It's time to go for it and thrive. Know you are necessary. Let God's will be done in your life.

Break FREE!

CHAPTER 6

Focus on You

Focus On You

Focus is to direct one's attention or efforts. You do your best when you focus on you. I noticed when I prepare my time, my food, and my week, I am more focused on what's in front of me. It takes a lot of energy to take care of your affairs.

****NEWS FLASH****

Make it your goal to live a quiet life, minding your own business and working with your hands, just as we instructed you before (1 Thessalonians 4:11-NLT).

Taking care of yourself is a full-time job. This is intentional living at its best. We confuse our lives with others and remove ourselves from our focus by comparing our lives with others. I heard this saying all the time, "If I had that then my life would be better." It could be comparing yourself to being married, having a house, a slim body, more money, other people's kids, a good job, etc. The reality is if God wanted you to have it, it would be yours. Learn to appreciate what's in front of you so, you don't have regrets because of how you mishandled your life.

I used to compare my life to others because of my upbringing or just because I wanted more. Why do we feel we need more because of what someone else has? You think you want it but you don't have a clue how they are handling their lives from day to day. So, what happened to me was I lost everything I had because I misappropriated my FOCUS. Why is that? I lost sight! I was so busy taking care of everyone else that I neglected my own household.

God had to grow me up fast. Imagine being in church and receiving a wonderful message on Mother's Day and as you were leaving you get a call that everything you owned was destroyed in a fire. All kinds of thoughts were running rampant in my mind. What in the world am I going to do? My son and I were homeless!

God had my undivided attention again. I had nowhere else to turn. Too many times I was taking my mask off to help other people, but I was dying inside. So, I had to develop a consciousness about my situation. I felt like I was lost spiritually, physically, and emotionally. I was completely broken.

God restored me. I had to learn how to redirect my focus on what was placed in front of me by surrendering to His way. Sometimes in life we lose focus because of the waves of distractions coming at us. He sent some amazing people in my life to help me get it together. Without them, I don't know where I would be! I was blessed with a sisterhood to develop my growth in God and pushed me to my next level.

Our job as women is to create a sisterhood to build each other up and not tear one another down. You should be able to go to your sister in confidence and not slander her (Proverbs 11:13). Cover her in prayer but to be jealous is a dangerous weapon for hatred!

Are you covering and building her up? Or revealing her weakness to the world such as social media, friends, or family? Think this through, ladies. Break free from this now and focus on you.

CHAPTER 7

Your Moment

Your Moment

Listen, you came into this world with lights overhead. You were crying and kicking, turning red. As a newborn you've been in the womb for nine months and to see the light and people is new. So, you squirm around knowing and unknowing what's going on and who am I? You were made with a cloth like none other. Everything about you is different from your eyes, your tone, your walk, your hands, and when you walk in the room you change the atmosphere because of who you are.

There would never be anyone like you. Your children may look, sound like you, or may have your mannerism, but it would never ever be another YOU! You are unique and necessary when God created you He put His best hand. You are it. Look yourself in the mirror and say, "I AM IT." You are the ONE. Since day one you have been it!

Now we have released ourselves from our past. The stage is ready for YOU. Walk with me and visualize the lights, camera, and action. The crew is setting up your stage with your name on it, the audience is waiting to be seated. The materials are being printed for your debut. The red carpet has been rolled out. Your glam squad is ready. Your loved ones are in the audience, cheering you on. You look in the mirror and encourage yourself and say, "IT'S MY TIME." The announcer is preparing to announce you to the world.

The audience can hear your footsteps walking to the stage. And the big announcement comes. PRESENTING… (insert your name). The adrenaline is pounding in your chest as you face your fears of walking in your destiny. BREAKING FREE OF WHAT HAS BOUND YOU.

The confidence of knowing that I was built for this. The reassurance of knowing that.

God has orchestrated this moment just for you. You were tailor made for this. It's your time.

Prayer, Scriptures, and References

My inspiration to write this book came from the following: The Holy Bible, NKJV, ESV, NLT, and NIV. Bishop T.D. Jakes' books (Instincts and Destiny) along with his teachings. Van Moody The People Factor. The Power of a Praying Woman, Dr. Myles Munroe, Pastor Ron Stephens (Temple Church of Christ), Coach Kim Burke Thomas (The Code). Lisa Nichols, Nikki Woods, Nicole Roberts Jones and much more.

This is my story of how I broke free from my old ways and thinking. It's my time and I'm walking into my destiny. The lights and cameras are ready and so am I. I don't just want to survive, I will THRIVE.

Enjoying this wave and inhaling all of HIS love and grace.

September 17, 2015, 12:58 p.m.

Focus On You

Here's the tools. Let's make note to identify a few areas of your life:

1. Who are you to you?
2. At what point in your life have you said to yourself or just stop "dreaming"
3. At what point did you lose you and why

<u>You are Victorious and an Overcomer. I believe in YOU.</u>

Meditate on this prayer and scriptures:

Father, thank you for loving us through it all! I pray you set (insert your name) free from the past. Release me from my past so I could move out of it and freely walk into my divine purpose for my life and enter into my future. I release my past to you, God, because only you can heal me, deliver me, and set me free from it! I'm no longer bound to the expectation of man but my desire is to please your heart! I have a purpose and with that I have no desire to want someone's life when You have given me my LIFE! All I have to ask and not covet (James 4:2). And thank you that You make all things new and that You are making me new in every way! (Revelations 21:5). Help me to put my FOCUS on where I am going and not where I have been. Forgetting what lies behind and straining forward to what lies ahead (Philippians 3:13). I honor You for all things are made new in YOU. In Jesus' name, Amen.

You are it!

Here are the tools.Let's make a note to identify a few areas of your life:

1. What are you willing to let go of in order to pursue your dreams?
2. Are you a procrastinator? If so, are you willing to free yourself from this?
3. Are you ready to maximize your moment?
4. Ask yourself, what am I afraid of? Face it; move forward.

<u>Meditate on this prayer and scriptures:</u>

Father, thank you for the gifts and the talents that you have given us. For you are a God that change not. Help us to just do those things that you've called me to do. Releasing the spirit of procrastinating what does it profit, if someone says he has faith but does not have works? Faith without works are dead (James 2:14-26). I know you are my God and You love me with all Your heart. And we know that all things work together for good to those who love God, to those who are called according to His purpose. (Romans 8:28) I'm ready, God, to write the book, build the business, teach, start my ministry, help the sick, promote my first album but I can't do it without you. I surrender all to you. In Jesus' name, Amen.

The Breaking Point

Here are the tools. Let's make note to identify a few areas of your life:

1. A wise man once told me you have to allow God to do the separating and be ok with that. You have to love them and leave them.
    a. Who has God removed from your life and you continuously keep going back? And why?
2. Have you prayed for your divine relationship?
3. Make a list of the people in your life and what's their purpose? What do they add to your life?

<u>Meditate on this prayer and scriptures:</u>

Father, thank you for you called us friend. Heal me from any past hurt from previous relationships. Lord, I lift up every one of my relationships to you and ask you to bless them richly. I refuse to force relationships to happen but allow them to happen by YOU. Give me discernment and strength to separate myself from anyone who is not a good influence. Teach me not to believe every spirit, but test the spirits whether they are of God (1 John 4:1). Also, let forgiveness and love flow deeply between us all. Make me be your light in all my relationships. In Jesus' name, Amen.

As I look back at all God has pulled my family, friends, and myself through…

It's possible to forgive It's possible to start over

It's possible to love again It's possible to let go

It's possible to stop overthinking It's possible to surrender

It's possible to meet the new you

It's possible to love the skin you are in It's possible to move forward

It's possible to walk in what's divinely yours It's possible to be the best you

It's possible to live your dreams

It's possible to start your business/ministry It's possible to reconcile

It's possible to be peaceful

It's possible to mind your own business It's possible to seek God in all you do

It's possible to be by yourself and never alone It's possible to be still in Him

It's possible to develop who you are in His word. One thing for sure through Him all things are possible!

Matthew 19:26b

A pivotal hour of my life came and
I surrendered all.

Thank You Letters

TO MY DAD

The art of forgiveness and love has been the key to our relationship.

The growth of your soul has been strength to my life.

Your love for me has allowed me to see and love God on another level.

Our relationship has been orchestrated by the hand of God.

He has a plan for your life and I've watched Him take you to heights that only He could.

Even when everyone had given up on you, I saw my daddy through it all.

I dreamed of the day of having a father and daughter relationship. Because of my obedience to God,. I'm reaping through honoring the gift of Him in you.

Thank you for being the man of God you were always destined to be.

TO MY MOM

Mom, the angel of your life was a reflection of me.

Your desire to save my life through hiding your pain.

The nights of not understanding THE WHY, you continue to raise your children through the misunderstanding.

The epiphany of your world was being formed.

Sick days, not enough money, medication needed, food low, disconnection notice and the lack of support.

Words cannot express how much I appreciate your level of love toward me!

The freedom to live in spite of the odds!

Your sacrifices pacing the floor, up praying all night, counting your change to prepare a meal and living off government assistance because of your many health issues.

Now it's your time to reap your harvest!

To all teen moms, moms, sisters, friends, and daughters

You are the light of the world, A lady of purpose and destiny. Your past is forgiven.

Do yourself a favor and forgive yourself.

No one can take what has been placed on this earth for you at your reach.

You are uniquely created and everything about you is sufficient and significant.

Noteworthy, worth waiting on, seeking after you through the trenches

God has purposely hidden you for someone special to search HIM for you.

Visualize being in a field seeking for a place of tranquility… you are it.

The nights of being up with sick kids, studying for an exam, washing clothes, caring for your sick parents, not understanding you're WHY……..He was preparing you for your best wine

He was changing you for the new wine skins. You are not the same person anymore.

Your destiny is asking for your permission to be a part of you empowering the world through your gift.

You are necessary! Wipe your face and smile. Now, look in the mirror and say I want more! Inhale and exhale that's your sign…. There's More In You.

Dear God

The art of knowing there's more to me has developed my faith in YOU! The better I is forming a creative mind to serve you more. My life's challenges were a product of your love toward me. You never took your hands off of me. You equipped me from the beginning to endure everything that was destined to come my way. You ensure me that I have a purpose in life. You didn't allow the harm I caused upon myself to forfeit my blessings/destiny. You protected me from the attacks I was unable to see. You covered me when I wanted revenge.

You reminded me of your love and forgiveness toward me. In the search of finding my voice, you built a bone thicker enough in my back to stand. You orchestrated the affliction and the persecution of my life. At the end of the day, you knew I would choose you. You put your love in my heart and gave me your word to exhibit it. I was never discovered on the stage but I was discovered serving, which has given me this opportunity for this stage now. You promised me what I do secretly I would be rewarded openly.

With so much gratitude and thanks in my heart, I share this moment with you. And to know you are well pleased with my worship has given me life. Your touch has changed my life. It will be amazing to know that I will leave my hand print on this earth by following your instruction to SERVE!

Karona "Kaye" Wilson

Inspired by: Imagery International

Founder Lady Eneazer Layne www.imageryintl.org

Moments of Reflections
"A 30 Day Journal"

DAY: 1

God gave you a gift of 86,400 seconds today. Have you used one to say **"Thank You?"** **Anonymous**

Day: 2

Don't lose HOPE! **Karona "Kaye" Wilson**

DAY: 3

"If you are working on something exciting that you really care about, you don't have to be pushed. The vision pulls you." **Steve Jobs**

DAY: 4

A man's gift makes room for him, and brings him before great men.
Proverbs 18:16 (NKJV)

DAY: 5

"What are you willing to let go in order to pursue your purpose in life?"
Karona "Kaye" Wilson

DAY: 6

For God gave us a spirit not of fear but of power and love and self-control. **2 Timothy 1:7 (ESV)**

DAY: 7

Finishing is better than starting. Patience is better than pride.
Ecclesiastes 7:8 (NLT)

DAY: 8

A friend loves at all times. **Proverbs 17:17a (NIV)**

DAY: 9

Life is a journey. Enjoy it! **Karona "Kaye" Wilson**

DAY: 10

Want to change your life? Change your way of thinking.
Karona "Kaye" Wilson

DAY: 11

Everything is possible for one who believes **Mark 9:23 (NIV)**

DAY 12:

"How you spent your time would be revealed in time."
Pastor Ron Stephens

Day: 13

Remain laser focused! **Karona "Kaye" Wilson**

Day: 14

If any of you lacks wisdom, you should ask God, who gives generously to all without finding fault, and it will be given to you. **James 1:5 (NIV)**

Day: 15

and to make it your ambition to lead a quiet life: You should mind your own business and work with your hands, just as we told you.
1 Thessalonians 4:11 (NIV)

Day: 16

Don't make excuses just make adjustments!
Karona "Kaye" Wilson

Day: 17

When your vision is honestly birthed by God Himself, He will be delighted to direct your steps. **Anonymous**

Day: 18

"Do you believe in YOU? If not, why not? You are necessary!"
Karona "Kaye" Wilson

Day: 19

"Forgivingness is a gift to us!" **Anonymous**

Day: 20

The Lord is good to those whose hope is in Him, to the one who seeks Him **Lamentations 3:25 (NIV)**

Day: 21

Don't allow your temper to keep you out of the promised land!
Anonymous

Day: 22

I'm not saying that I have this all together, that I have it made. But I am well on my way, reaching out for Christ, who has so wondrously reached out for me. Friends, don't get me wrong: By no means do I count myself an expert in all of this, but I've got my eye on the goal, where God is beckoning us onward—to Jesus. I'm off and running, and I'm not turning back. **Philippians 3:13-14 (MSG)**

Day: 23

Pray. Take action. Pray. **Karona "Kaye" Wilson**

Day: 24

Stop telling people more than they need to know.
Karona "Kaye" Wilson

Day: 25

Be faithful in the small opportunities. Begin where you are and do what you can, and leave the results to God. He rejoices to see the work begin. **Zechariah 4:10**

Day: 26

"Integrity is doing the right thing even when no one is watching."
C.S. Lewis

Day: 27

What then shall we say to these things? If God *is* for us, who *can be* against us? **Romans 8:31(NKJV)**

Day: 28

Ask me and I will tell you remarkable secrets you do not know about things to come. **Jeremiah 33:3 (NLT)**

Day: 29

But seek first the kingdom of God and His righteousness, and all these things shall be added to you. **Matthew 6:33 (NKJV)**

Day: 30

You are worth fighting for! God hears and sees you! There's More In YOU!!! **Karona "Kaye" Wilson**

About the Author

Karona "Kaye" Wilson is the owner of the St. Louis-based K.W. Hair Designs. She is a servant, motivator, educator, mentor, entrepreneur, hair designer, author, and a friend to many. She has poured into so countless other lives throughout the years by sharing her story. From the salon chair to one-on-one sessions and packed audiences, as a distributor with Juice Plus+, a whole food based nutrition, Wilson stands on the mantra, "Everything I do is rooted in my belief!"

Also, she has facilitated women's empowerment groups and life-skill classes for teen moms at Almost Home, an organization that empowers young women to become self-sufficient in order to create a better future for themselves and their children.

Wilson has collaborated as a hairstylist with local companies such as The Perfect Wedding Guide, Alive Magazine, Curls with a Cause, and Missouri Style Week. Additionally, her industry connections have allowed her to expand into editorial work and enhanced her knowledge of branding and advertising. Beyond her expertise on outward beauty, she also focuses on awakening one's inner beauty through inspirational and motivational speaking. As a role model, she has been able to uplift others by delivering her story. Being willing to serve others through her passion and love for the craft has been the key to her success. It is through disclosing and believing that "it's possible" in everything she does, that she is able to say, "Live Your Dream."

St. Louis, Missouri, is where she resides with her son.

To book Wilson for speaking engagements, visit her website www.theresmoreinyou.com

I BELIEVE THERE'S MORE IN YOU!

Made in the USA
Middletown, DE
01 August 2017